Listenings

Listenings
Meditations for Everyone

by
Andrew Costello

THE THOMAS MORE PRESS
Chicago, Illinois

ISBN 0-88347-119-1

TABLE OF CONTENTS

LISTENINGS

Meditations for Everyone

Everyone has the same joys.

Everyone has the same needs.

Everyone has the same problems.

I suppose that's the biggest discovery I've made so far in the journey of life. We all seem to be on the same road, the same stage together. Of course Shakespeare said all this far better than me. But he too was one of us. "All the world's a stage. . . ."

The following are thoughts and images jotted down in the dressing room after being out there on the stage with people in counseling, parties, planes, and at coffee breaks.

In the middle ages there was a play called *Everyman*. The hope was that everyman—men and women—while watching the play would identify with the main character, Everyman. (Every*one* we would say today.)

The plot was simple. Everyman is standing there on the stage enjoying life. Suddenly a character named Death appears on stage, walks up to Everyman and announces, "Your time is up. It's time for the reckoning."

Well, when I heard that, when I saw Everyman panic as if he had to deal not only with his death, but also with his whole life I really began to think. I began to meditate on the big question of life.

The same thing is happening to me on the stage of everyday life. As I listen to people's stories I often hear them telling my story.

The following then are meditations. They are my way of reporting what I'm hearing everyone going through.

They are listenings.

Andrew Costello, C. SS.R.

PART ONE
Everyone

TIME OUT

Everyone of us needs to call
      "Time out,"
        from the game of life.

If we don't, we're in a rat race,
      running and running,
      in a marathon
      that's going nowhere.

Everyone needs to take time out
      to see where we are,
      and where our roads,
      where our decisions,
      and non-decisions
      are taking us.

Everyone must look to Jesus,
        the Way,
        the one who took the time out
        to go into the desert,
        to wrestle with the temptations of life,
        to pray to know the Father's will.

Everyone must be like Jesus
        and every once and a while
        spend a night alone
        on a mountain in communion
        with the Father.

Otherwise, when we find ourselves
        in the garden of despair
        because of rejections,
        or cancer,
        or a sudden death,
        we won't know the Father's will,
        we won't be able to reach for His cup
        like a runner in the race.

EVERY PERSON

Every person is a gift shop
      along the turnpike
      with open doors,
      with shelves of gifts
      like open arms,
      hoping to attract
      every traveler.

Every person is a TV set
      with an on-off button.

Every person is a newspaper,
      or better the Sunday paper,
      with all kinds of sections:
      comics,
      sports,
      fashions,
      tragedies,
      obituaries,
      advertisements,
      the latest news

to be looked at,
news that everybody
in the house
wants to read,
sometimes.

Every person is a tree,
with roots,
with leaves,
with blossoms,
with fruit,
that change
with the seasons.

Every person is a slide show
with pictures taken
from many trips,
in many places,
with many friends.

Every person is a tray of hors d'oeuvres
ready to be tasted,
ready to be savored.

Every person is a menu,
including a cocktail
before supper.

Every person is waiting
to sit down to supper
with you and me.

TALKING TO ONESELF

Everyone needs to talk to oneself,
        to walk with oneself,
        when walking the dog,
        when driving the car,
        along the city streets,
        walking the quiet beach,
        or in June and November woods.

Everyone needs to meet with oneself,
        to make plans,
        decisions,
        all by oneself,
        when all are talking,
        at the card party,
        or the coffee break
        or outside the church.

We all need to slip in the side door
        of ourselves,
        or our church,
        and sit in
        the afternoon darkness,
        and hear the Light,
        feel the Light
        that surrounds us.

And even then we all need moments
        to get away
        even from God,
        to hide in the cellar
        and the caves
        of our hearts,
        our secret spots
        of wilderness
        and quiet.

We all need those times
        to cry,
        to die,
        to tie things together.

Yes, we all need time to talk to ourselves,
        to rent a boat,
        to leave the beach,
        to row out beyond the world,
        to find some quiet time,
        to stop the stirring
        of the coffee cup
        and just let it sit still,
        and let the waves,
        and then the ripple,
        and then the Calm
        surround us.

TARGETS

All of us have our own dartboards
         and pool tables
         and ping pong tables
         deep in our cellars,
         deep in our hearts.

And each move we make,
         each word we say,
         we aim to win,
         we aim to get our point across,
         to get ourselves across,
         to control the game.

We aim to sink our ideas,
         our images,
         our perceptions,
         into the side pocket
         of another,
         to hit the bull's eye,
         to win the game.

But all of us do this so differently,
        having our own style of play,
        our own way.

Some of us come right out
        and say what we mean,
        and mean what we say,
        aiming right at the target,
        on the offensive,
        on the attack,
        so assertive,
        in the games called
        meetings,
        dinners,
        relationships,
        at home
        or at the corner bar.

But some of us are tricky,
        waiting back,
        playing defensively,
        being quiet at the coffee break,
        asking questions,
        listening,
        receiving,
        but always trying
        to control the action,
        control the game,
        always trying to win,
        to be number one.

PHOTO ALBUM

Everyone of us can find ourselves
      on the pages
      of the New Testament.

It is our photo album,
      our biography,
      the story of our lives.

I am the blind man
      wanting to see,
      needing to cry out,
      "Son of David, have pity on me."

I am the Prodigal Son
        far away from the Father,
        longing for the pleasures of distant lands,
        yet longing for the comforts of home.

I am the Pharisee, the phony,
        seeing specks in my brother's eye,
        and blind to the planks in my own.

Oh yes, at times I'm the Good Samaritan,
        helping my brothers and sisters
        lying by the side of the road.
        But so many times I find myself
        as Pontius Pilate washing my hands
        of all responsibility.

I am the lost sheep,
        the lost coin,
        forgetting I've been branded,
        been stamped with the sign of the cross.

I must learn to read
        the letters of Paul and John
        as if they were addressed to me,
        put in my mailbox,
        so that I'll begin to bear
        the other's burdens,
        and discover that God is Love.

I must discover that the Messiah, the Christ,
        has entered my village,
        and today wants to eat at my house.

THE HOUSE

All of us live in this enormous house
     high on the hill,
     a house filled
     with room
     after room
     after room.

And some of us eat and sleep
     and love and work
     and wonder
     and listen
     in those rooms.

And some of us walk the corridors
     wondering what's going on
     inside those rooms.

And some of us get angry
        at the voices
        in the rooms below,
        waking up
        in the night
        with the barking of a dog
        or the flushing of a toilet.

And some of us play there
        with cards,
        or Monopoly,
        or Scrabble
        with the words of life.

And some of us feel all alone
        as in a womb
        sitting in corners,
        watching the phone,
        looking out windows,
        always waiting
        and waiting
        and waiting.

But most of us are deaf; we don't realize
        that Jesus is standing there,
        knocking on the door, saying,
        "If anyone hears me calling
        and opens the door, I will enter
        his house and have supper with him,
        and he with me."

EMERGENCY ROOM

Deep inside ourselves,
    each of us
    needs an emergency room,
    a place to go,
    to heal and be healed
    of all our inner wounds
    and sores,
    and all those cuts
    we slash on ourselves.

All of us have to practice
    getting there,
    taking care
    of all those times
    we look at ourselves
    with disgust and guilt,

and rip the photograph
of ourselves in two
and throw ourselves
into the garbage,
wishing we didn't say
what we said,
or do what we did,
always seeing the photo
of another as better,
never accepting ourselves,
our accidents,
our sins.

And so we constantly
        break the news to ourselves,
        that these inner cuts,
        these inner abortions,
        these self massacres,
        are beyond the healing hands
        of Jesus,
        of friends,
        of family,
        constantly
        forgetting
        that they are one of us.

And so we overeat,
        and overreact,
        and overhate,
        and overkill,
        ourselves.

THE OLD NEWSPAPER

All of us are newspaper reporters,
    telling our story,
    selling our story,
    trying to catch
    the other's eye,
    reporting to others
    that we've been to Europe and Hawaii,
    that we have two kids in college
    and three grandchildren,
    that we have a cousin in California
    with a $250,000 home,
    and therefore please read
    that I'm okay,
    that I'm not a failure.

And sometimes when we begin
    to really trust another reader,
    we begin to report our failures,
    our sad stories,
    about our kids who dropped out,
    about divorces and drinking
    in the family,
    and how it all makes us feel so small.

And all of us know
        what it feels like
        to be misread,
        or what's worse,
        to be rejected,
        to have someone
        just look at our headlines
        and then be thrown onto a pile,
        or to be used to wrap the garbage
        or for cat litter.

And all of us are part of every robbery and rape,
        and all those stories
        in Dear Abby or Dear Ann,
        stories of wives being used,
        and husbands being rejected,
        and teen-agers being sent to bed
        right in the middle of their
        favorite TV show,
        story after story of insensitivity.

And all of us know the feeling
        of being used as paper
        to line the bottom drawer,
        hoping that someday,
        somebody will pick us up and say,
        "Hey, look at this old paper.
        Let's see what it has to say."

DIPLOMATS

All of us are diplomats,
        traveling with
        our portfolios,
        our interests,
        wheeling and dealing,
        salesmen of self,
        sending signals,
        waiting for replies,
        announcing to the world,
        "Here I am!
        You are going to have to
        deal with me."

All of us are space makers,
        place makers,
        trying to carve out
        our territory,
        trying to protect
        our interests,
        our marriages,
        our lives.

All of us are committed.

All of us are dedicated.

All of us are religious.

But that's not the issue.

The obvious question is:
>What are we religious about?
>What do we wrap our time around?
>What are we after?

Is it self
>approval,
>acceptance,
>control,
>for me,
>for you,
>for God?

All of us are diplomats,
>shuttling back and forth
>words and messages,
>about who we are
>and what we want.

But have we ever examined
>the contents
>of our briefcase?

SHOW AND TELL

Why do we all have this urge
        to confess
        to tell another
        about our eerie doings,
        about our collisions,
        to give a blow by blow account
        of all our dark ramblings into sin?

Why do we all need to vomit out
        our overeating,
        especially from another's plate,
        from another's life?

Why do we hunt for bars
        for some person
        with understanding ears,
        ash tray cleaners
        who will dump our fears
        into the garbage
        and place our lives nice and clean
        back on the bar?

Why can't we forget these oil spills
        floating on the surface
        of our lives as we lie there
        fascinated by these greasy rainbows?

Why can't we simply forgive ourselves,
        and stop picking the scab,
        never letting our cuts heal,
        always looking for someone
        to look at our cuts and sores?

Why do we have this compulsion to find someone
        we can confess to,
        to announce to,
        that we have adulterated our lives?

Isn't it all a confession
        of our need for You, O Jesus?

SKIN DEEP

Everyone is skin that
        gets touched,
        gets cut,
        gets neglected,
        gets burned,
        gets loved.

Everyone is skin that
        needs Vasoline,
        needs bandages,
        needs caring,
        needs the loving touch.

Everyone is skin that
            packages
            and contains
            and holds
            a vast organization
            of memories,
            of nerves,
            of thoughts,
            of feelings,
            of wonderings.

Everyone is skin that
            blushes,
            and pains,
            and vibrates
            with joy,
            when one
            is accepted,
            and loved,
            and welcomed
            into the group,
            the family.

Everyone is skin that
            scars,
            and wrinkles,
            and gets old,
            and finally
            dies and
            is boxed away
            deep into
            the earth
            from which
            it was formed.
            by God.

DEATH

Everyone of us must face death.
        Let's face it.
        It comes moving in
        like the weather
        and no one
        can escape the report.

All of us must face death,
        our own
        and that of our friends,
        mother, father,
        brothers, sisters,
        wives and nephews,
        the whole family.

And we'll all get a marker
saying we were here,
flowers,
prayers,
tears,
a notice in the paper,
a wake,
moments at the grave,
and then the memories.

Everybody knows it and everybody
has written about it,
and all of us still
keep the thought of it
in a bottom drawer,
in a box
with a rubber band
around it.

But it comes creeping out,
seeping out,
asking us
on a regular basis,
the regular question.

What are we going to do about it?

AVOIDING CHANGE

None of us really want to break
    the dollar bill
    and have all
    that loose change
    sitting around
    in our pocket.

Coins can be lost so easily,
    slipping out of our pockets,
    but that dollar bill
    can sit so still and soft
    and safe in our wallets.

Who really wants to change?

We all get mad when the stranger
    at the toll booth
    gives us all those coins,
    when he could have given us
    a dollar bill instead.

Who really wants to change?

We want it the way it is,
            our way,
            our will,
            our style,
            and so we walk away,
            we don't listen,
            we stab others
            in the back
            who want change,
            these strangers,
            these givers
            of the unexpected,
            who hand us a bunch of coins,
            when we expected a dollar bill.

Change. Who really wants to start carrying around
            a new way,
            the unexpected?

But didn't life start
            and spread
            by clusters of cells,
            like coins,
            getting together
            in the pockets
            of the earth,
            changing,
            and changing,
            and changing,
            change?

TRUCK DRIVERS HAVE FEELINGS TOO

Everyone is a truck driver,
     carrying feelings
     across state lines,
     carrying hurts,
     carrying joys,
     ice cream and salt,
     everywhere he goes.

Everyone moves down highways,
     transporting
     the memories
     of yesterday,
     the digs,
     the hurts,
     the cuts,
     the remarks,
     the jokes,
     the good days
     and the bad,
     everywhere she goes.

Everyone has accidents,
       dents,
       wrong turns,
       gets lost,
       feels stupid,
       is scared to ask for directions,
       and finally gets his strength back
       from his fellow drivers
       back at the diner.

Everyone has gifts to deliver,
       products to sell,
       stops to make,
       and sometimes she's late.

Everyone has hills to climb,
       roads to travel,
       and often is surrounded
       and frustrated
       by other people,
       driving at different speeds,
       with different feelings
       on their minds.

And everyone runs out of gas.

IT'S IN THE CARDS

All of us are card players,
       sitting there,
       playing there,
       dealing there,
       wondering what's going on
       in another's hand,
       in another's life,
       in the other's heart.

And at times we all get a chance
        to play the king or queen,
        or the lowly two of hearts,
        and at times
        we love to play the joker.

Cards teach us how to win
        and how to lose
        and how to play the game.

And sometimes we sit there
        kicking ourselves
        under the table,
        for making the wrong move,
        for playing the wrong card,
        and we continue to think about
        our "stupid mistakes",
        the rest of the night,
        the rest of our lives.

Cards.

Some play for money,
        some for fun,
        some, the real ones
        play for people,
        holding them in their hands,
        holding them in their hearts.

HUNGERS AND THIRSTS

To be
To be born
To walk
To talk
To be held
To be taught
To be understood.

For food
For family
For caring
For trust
For satisfaction
For friendship
For recognition.

To share
To serve
To be asked
To think
To speak
To be noticed
To be heard.

For dreams
For justice
For peace
For laughter
For music
For meaning
For the Kingdom of God.

To risk
To love
To go beyond the valley
To climb the hill
To die
To rise
To embrace the Father.

HOPELESS CASES

Each of us has to deal with hopeless cases,
      with people we know
      who "drive us up the wall",
      who "could drive us to drink",
      who "drive us crazy",
      as all those pet phrases go
      that describe people
      who are hard to take.

First there are the wives
      who have to deal with husbands
      who are married to their jobs,
      husbands who mean by "baby"
      their latest project,
      at work,
      at the club,
      or at the church,
      or all three,
      who finally come home at night
      and make love
      to the newspaper,
      to the TV,
      to silence.

Then there are the husbands
        whose wives are married
        to their children,
        to their mothers,
        to themselves,
        and the divorce comes
        long before the papers.

Then there are the workers
        who have bosses
        who move up the ladder
        by stepping on the hands
        of those on the rungs below,
        who don't listen,
        who don't care,
        who don't examine
        the way they treat others.

Let's be honest. Each of us has a list
        of at least three people,
        usually relatives,
        or at least in-laws,
        whom we consider hopeless cases.

Why? Why do we make it so tough
        for each other?
        Why can't I figure out
        whose list I'm on?
        Why can't I be the first one to change?

ADVICE

At times we all feel stuck
        and small and all alone,
        caught in a pool of stagnation,
        of stupidity,
        because of sex,
        or money,
        or parents,
        or spouse,
        or people at work,
        or something we can't even describe.

And at times we all start looking around us,
        for a way out,
        for the right person,
        to yell to for help,
        someone on the solid ground
        around the grassy edge
        of the pool of stagnation,
        someone who will listen,
        someone who will understand,
        someone who will put everything all right,
        The Outsider.

So we call to the Clergy,
        the Psychologist,
        the Best Friend,
        somebody in the family,
        anybody who will give us a hand
        and lift us out of the pool of stagnation.

Sometimes these help.

Sometimes people even turn to God.

But then as the days slip by,
        as I find myself
        sliding back into the pool of stagnation,
        I begin to realize
        that decisions are up to me,
        that yes I have to work
        with the love,
        and grace,
        the advice of others.

But I'm the one in charge of my life,
        the Insider.

SHOPPING CART

All of us meditate
        all the time,
        making the salad,
        setting the table,
        driving the car,
        painting the chair,
        knitting the sweater,
        putting together
        the fabric of our lives.

All of us wonder
        all the time,
        in buses,
        planes,
        trains,
        while waiting in line
        at the bank.

All of us keep turning over new ground,
        planting new plants,
        new hopes,
        new thoughts,
        new flowers,
        new possibilities,
        about our lives
        and the events that surround us.

All of us give ourselves
        our own tests,
        and own marks,
        and then take home
        our own report card every day,
        and sometimes worry about it
        deep into the night.

All of us watch the rain run down the window
        and watch the wet streets,
        the mailman,
        the wedding,
        the funeral,
        and a thousand other things each day.

All of us meditate all day long,
        thinking all day long,
        putting all kinds of things
        into our shopping carts,
        from all kinds of shelves,
        but do we really want to think
        about all these things.
        Do we really want to buy them?

Do we want all these groceries in our cart?

Have we ever really heard Jesus' parable of the net?

VISION CENTER

All of us are looking and searching
        for a vision center,
        for the answer to the question
        of the meaning of our lives.

So we go to temples,
        universities,
        psychiatrists,
        astrologists,
        book stores,
        buying fads,
        trying movements,
        looking for answers
        to our quest,
        looking for the Way,
        the Truth and the Life.

Some of us think the center is
        Washington, Moscow or Peking,
        Mecca, Rome or Jerusalem,
        Paris, Hollywood or New York City,
        always searching
        for the center of life,
        fashion, style, money,

politics, power, dance,
forgetting that the veil
of the temple
has been cut in two,
forgetting that the kingdom
of God is within.

Some of us stop along the highway
at those buildings marked,
"Adult Books and Movies,"
"For Mature Audiences Only,"
and only years later
come out wondering
what maturity
and being an adult
is all about.

All of us then are tiny ships
making for harbors
in the night,
leaving at dawn and
launching out into the deep,
lowering our nets
for a catch,
for the Center.

All of us keep looking.
Wise men and women,
following the star,
journeying towards
the Center of the Universe.

THE PRESSURE

All of us must walk the streets,
        the valleys,
        and walk beyond
        where we are
        right now,
        till we find a porch
        and a rocking chair,
        both within ourselves
        and without.

All of us must journey
        beyond the edge
        of our everyday boundaries,
        following,
        but mainly deciding,
        the turns
        of our road
        from birth till death.

All of us must step beyond
        our jobs,
        our duties,
        our burnt out buildings,
        and vacation
        by our inner streams
        and waterfalls.

All of us must stop at service stations
        along the road
        to get a map,
        or ask our fellow travelers
        where we are
        and where we want to go
        and if anybody knows the Way.

We all need to silence ourselves,
        to still ourselves,
        to space out,
        to space in,
        and even though
        the others ask,
        "Where is she?"
        "Is he praying again?"
        "What's wrong with her?"
        to keep walking along,
        even though
        we walk with
        the Pressure.

THE BEST THING THAT EVER HAPPENED TO ME

All of us contain the best thing
    that ever happened to us.

Did anybody ever ask you that question?
    "What was the best thing
    that ever happened to you?"

A radio station in New York City
    gives twenty-five dollars
    for the answer.

We all hold the answer to the question
    somewhere inside of us,
    in our file system.

We hold the memory of the day
        we won the boy or girl
        that we always wanted,
        or won the race,
        or the scholarship,
        or decided to quit the job,
        or move and start again.

Or it might have been
        that second honeymoon
        to the Bahamas,
        or simply a week-end
        away from the kids,
        or a quiet retreat
        by the shore.

We all have our inner vault,
        where we bank
        not only the terrors of life,
        the deaths and disappointments,
        but also all those right moments
        that changed our lives.

And like being asked our favorite movie or song,
        after a little effort,
        we can all name
        the most important day
        of our life.

It might have been a Columbus-like
        self-discovery
        and maybe someday
        it might contain God.

THE SPIDER'S WEB

Sin is a spider's web
          that none of us notice
          till the morning
          after a night of darkness,
          a web that can catch
          and hold
          and kill us.

But when we decide to crawl in darkness
          we never notice the web.
          We step on others.
          We fly around like insects
          stinging our neighbors,

rationalizing our patterns,
overeating and overdrinking,
flirting with infidelities,
being jealous and envious,
piling up treasures for ourselves,
upsetting the balance of nature,
ruining the atmosphere around us,
forgetting the poor
and the sick and the aged,
putting ourselves in the center,
forgetting about God
and family and friends
and the rest of the world,
and finally we wake up
in the morning,
in the center,
the center of the web.

And as we hang there caught
in the morning,
in the light,
we start blaming others
for the web we're in,
looking for scapegoats,
others to blame,
and then we have the option,
the choice,
to confess our stupidity
and cry for help,
or to die
caught in our sins.

PAY PHONE

Everyone knows God is calling them,
    dialing them,
    trying to reach them,
    from a pay phone
    along the highway.

And everybody knows it's smart
    to be deaf,
    or to say,
    "Sorry, wrong number,"
    or, "I'm busy now."

Everybody knows God is a troublemaker,
    a changer of lives,
    a disrupter of temples,
    and so we keep God
    in churches,
    or in statues,
    or in cemetaries,
    but rarely in our lives.

It's much easier to sit still in a warm house
    in an easy chair,
    with a fireplace,
    and the papers or TV
    and let the phone
    keep ringing
    and ringing
    and ringing.

After all, who wants to have to go out traveling
    on a dark night
    to find out just where God is
    and what is wanted?

THE FOREST

All of us need to do some stopping
    from time to time,
    along the back trails
    of self, and figure out
    where we are
    and where we want to be.

All of us need to stop and sit
    on a rock,
    in the deep forest of self,
    to check our maps
    or look for the North Star.

All of us need to make some bold moves,
    to move out of our moods
    and the semi-darkness,
    and do some listening
    to all the voices
    we're really listening to,
    and make some choices
    out of the forces
    in our lives.

And all of us need to know that the forest
    is filled with people,
    as the night
    is filled with stars,
    people with answers
    to the questions
    in our lives.

And all of us need to leave that forest
    of self
    and make our move
    towards the City.

LOVE AND DEATH

Let's face it.
Let's cliche it.
Everybody knows it.

The two major issues of life are:
    Love and Death.

Yes, you can have one without the other,
    but when you do
    it's hell.

There is no greater love than this:
    to lay down one's life
    for one's friends.

Love and Death:
    the plot of every novel and movie,
    the story of everyone's life.

Husbands and wives,
    fathers and mothers,
    dying to self
    to love one another,
    serving their children
    all over the world.

People volunteering time and money
and themselves,
teaching, healing
and helping one another,
all over the world.

Love and Death:
the undercurrents,
the underlying themes of life.

Imagine walking along the cold, icy floor
of death without love,
and imagine all the people
who leap into the canyon of despair,
who try to self-destruct and die,
when they discover a relationship
or a marriage died,
because the love they thought
was there wasn't,
or what's worse, has died.
Another ice age.

O God of Love,
help us to die to self,
get us out of our chairs
and start us climbing
the hill for others.

THE JOURNEY

After nine long months we all land
    like astronauts
    on this earth
    with empty hands,
    and all the world
    watches for that first step.

First it's the stretching,
    then the crawling,
    then the leaning
    on a table,
    then the falling,
    then the standing,
    then that first step,
    then the second,
    and all applaud.

And soon like astronauts
        we begin collecting
        pieces of earth,
        pound after pound,
        first food and toys,
        then money from grandmothers,
        diplomas and degrees,
        friends here and there,
        and then more of the stuff of earth.

But before our mission is complete,
        like experienced travelers
        we learn the hard way
        what to leave behind,
        how to let go,
        to take only what
        is essential.

We learn by our mistakes,
        that our hands,
        our arms,
        our suitcases,
        our souls,
        our space ship,
        can carry only so much.

Then at the last minute,
        we hear the announcement
        that all we can take back
        is ourselves,
        just as we arrived
        with empty hands.

CHILDHOOD

Everyone of us is a child
        needing to be nursed,
        and held and loved
        and taught how
        to walk and talk,
        but mainly needing
        to learn how to wait.

Everyone of us is a child
        reaching for toys
        and playgrounds
        beyond our reach.

Everyone of us is a child
        waiting to be noticed
        in the morning,
        in the afternoon,
        in the night.

Everyone of us is a child
       waiting for birthdays,
       and holidays,
       and parties,
       and presents,
       and every kind
       of sign of love.

Everyone of us is a child
       that can't wait
       to go to school,
       and then can't wait
       to come home,
       and then wants
       to go out,
       promising to be back by
       5 o'clock,
       7 o'clock,
       9 o'clock,
       11 o'clock,
       midnight.

And then suddenly
       we find ourselves
       in our second childhood,
       in the homes of our children,
       in nursing homes,
       waiting for love,
       waiting,
       and waiting.

THE BIG TABLE

The whole world is seated
    at one big table,
    but the trouble is
    all the food
    is on one side.

The whole world is seated
    at one big table,
    but the trouble is
    people have problems
    passing things.

The whole world is seated
    at one big table,
    but the trouble is
    people have difficulties
    stomaching each other.

The whole world is seated
    at one big table,
    but the trouble is
    the first are first
    and the last are last.

The whole world is seated
        at one big table,
        but the trouble is
        people don't like
        the seating arrangements.

The whole world is seated
        at one big table,
        but the trouble is
        people seem to want
        separate tables.

The whole world is seated
        at one big table,
        but the trouble is
        nobody realizes
        the table is round.

The whole world is seated
        at one big table,
        but the trouble is
        the next generation
        is waiting for the leftovers.

THE RAFT

Somewhere out there in the deep waters
        is a raft
        called Love,
        called God.

And everybody knows it's there,
        somewhere,
        as we all swim
        around in this ocean
        of words and stuff,
        trying to find the raft
        called Love,
        knowing that Love
        is the answer,
        as all the songs sing it,
        as all the prophets tell us.

And it's hard work swimming and struggling
        and trying to find that raft
        called Love,
        called·God.

And suddenly some of us
         spot the raft
         off there in the distance
         and as we swim closer
         we see it's almost sinking
         with people.

Then God reaches out with his hands
         and pulls us up
         out of the water
         and onto the wood,
         and just then
         God suddenly laughs,
         watching us trying
         to lug our wet possessions
         on board, too.

But then God starts to clap
         and slaps somebody
         on the back,
         who just then saw our stupidity
         and threw his stuff overboard,
         and once more
         there is just enough room,
         just enough space,
         on the raft
         called Love,
         called God.

TO LIFE

Everyone is called to life,
      to dance the dance,
      to sing the song,
      to clap to the music
      of life.

Everyone is called to climb
      the ladder,
      to ride the slide,
      like children
      in a playground,
      enjoying every minute
      of the gift of life.

Everyone is called to enjoy snow
      and swimming,
      and taking children
      to the beach,
      to buy them candy,
      and watch their eyes sparkle
      when you surprise them
      with a double scoop of ice cream.

Everyone is called to dream the dream,
to build the house,
to work the tools,
to sew together
the fabric of life.

Everyone is called to learn
how to whistle,
and how to cook,
and how to tell the joke.

Everyone is called to play cards,
put on plays,
and sports,
and festivals,
and worship,
to celebrate
the gift of life.

In other words,
everyone
is called to enjoy
the meal of life,
to sit down
with each other
knowing that everyone
is invited
to life.

KITCHEN CALENDAR

Silently the calendar hangs there
    on the kitchen wall
    watching us all eat,
    listening to us
    plan our days.

Calendars, like clocks, keep reminding us,
    telling us,
    that we only have so much time,
    so many days.

But isn't the calendar more dramatic
    than the clock,
    sort of like the old hour glass
    that those now in graves
    used to watch,
    grains of sand
    flowing from the future,
    slipping through the fingers
    of the present,
    and falling down dead
    into the past.

And so at the end of each month
        we crumble up
        a piece of paper
        that listed
        appointments,
        holidays,
        birthdays,
        funerals,
        marriages,
        worst days,
        best days,
        and deadlines.

And then each January First,
        we bury the old calendar
        from the kitchen
        and put up a new one,
        knowing that for somebody
        in the house
        this year might be the last.

This one might contain a death day
        and so we open the refrigerator
        trying to think of something else.

BOX OF EXPECTATIONS

Everyone is a box of expectations,
    a box of hopes,
    waiting for letters,
    for phone calls,
    for the door bell,
    waiting for love.

Everyone hopes for the raise,
    the promotion,
    to be shop steward,
    to be next in line
    to be union delegate,
    to get a degree,
    to get a job,
    to get the title,
    to be the doctor,
    to be the nurse,
    to be the boss.

Everyone stands in the batter's box
    on the foul line,
    at the corner,
    hoping to score.

Everyone goes to the movies
        hoping to be moved,
        goes to bingo
        hoping to win,
        the race,
        the lottery,
        the big car,
        the grand prize.

Everyone is a shopper,
        searching,
        looking,
        reading,
        for meaning,
        for vision,
        reaching
        for her star,
        for his dream.

And suddenly everyone finds herself
        waiting for the baby,
        the child,
        the family,
        the reason for living,
        the reason for working.

Everyone is expecting,
        pregnant with hopes,
        pregnant with God.

SINK

All of us need sinks
        with faucets
        and drains,
        and soap,
        and water,
        and space,
        to wash away
        the hurts,
        the mistakes
        of everyday.

All of us stand there
      in the morning,
      in the evening,
      during the day,
      behind closed doors,
      and every once
      in awhile
      we really look
      into that mirror
      above the sink,
      and really look
      at the me
      I am.

All of us need that time
      at our sinks,
      to turn over
      a bar of soap
      in our hands,
      time to turn
      over a remark,
      or a wondering,
      or a relationship,
      in this place backstage,
      to think.

And then we can step back
      from the sink,
      dry off our hands
      and our face,
      and then adjust
      our masks,
      as we open the door
      and head back
      towards the stage.

AUTOBIOGRAPHY

All of us are writing our own book,
  our own story,
  our autobiography,
  chapter after chapter.

And the story contains every page
  of our lives,
  our parents,
  our family,
  and all the people and places
  we've touched so far.

And the first and most obvious thing
  we all would like to do
  is to rip out certain passages
  of our book,
  stories that sound so stupid,
  stories about broken relationships
  and sex,
  but we know
  we can't tear out
  anything that is part
  of the pages of our life.

And then there are those sections
        we keep re-reading
        getting angrier each time,
        sections where we've been hurt
        or rejected by parents or lovers
        or accidents that scarred us,
        sections that blur possibilities
        for our tomorrows,
        because we can't forgive
        our yesterdays.

And every once in awhile
            we have to sit back from our desks,
            and ask ourselves
            the significant questions,
            the meaning questions:
            What's the plot?
            Am I doing all this for myself
            or for others?
            Am I growing older
            but not growing up?
            Does the God of Love,
            the Lord Jesus,
            appear in the pages of my life?
            Is my story just happening
            or am I making it happen?
            Who am I writing this book for?

ANOTHER EAR

We all need to know another person
        is here with us,
        at least one other person
        who cares that we are here.

It's lonely to only listen to oneself,
        to only hear one's own words
        and that from the inside.

We need to speak to others
        and to know
        that we are heard,
        that we count,
        that we belong,
        that we make a difference.

We need another, at least one other,
    who not only sits there
    and hears us,
    but someone who tries
    to get beneath our words,
    who goes underneath our questions
    with questions to try to find out
    what we're really saying,
    perhaps sharing feelings
    we're too scared
    to even share with ourselves.

The world needs people who know
    how to shut up and listen,
    not just with silence,
    that can mean anything,
    but who really hear
    another's heart.

The world needs people who can stop
    this non-stop monologue
    we're all engaged in,
    who can break this chain
    of deaf people,
    with the sign language
    of listening,
    the language of God.

TEMPTATIONS

Everyone of us must eventually wrestle with
     the questions,
     the issues,
     the temptations of life.

We begin with the easy ones,
     the grabbing and the shoving,
     the fighting over toys,
     and move onto clothes and sex,
     and then like prodigals
     we move away from parents
     drugging ourselves on sleep
     or music or drink
     or the dozens of other
     adolescent seductions.

Till finally we find ourselves
     in a desert,
     in an exodus
     from the stupidity
     of our earlier statements
     about the meaning of life.

And there we begin to feel the Wind of God
        sweeping over the dry sand of our lives,
        there we begin to face,
        but this time with honesty,
        the religious traditions
        that were handed down to us,
        there we begin to be silent,
        to be objective towards ourselves,
        to get beyond mediocre temptations,
        to see causes and concerns outside ourselves,
        and finally to allow God to come into our temple
        and have him clean it out,
        till it becomes a house of prayer
        and not a den of thieves.

Then we can stand up straight,
        ready to move back into life,
        ready to be of service,
        to bear each other's burdens,
        knowing that the real struggle,
        the real temptation will now begin,
        the temptation to pin God down,
        knowing that like the wind
        He'll laugh as he rips
        the veil of our temple in two
        and the Wind of God
        will fill the world.

LORD, THAT I MIGHT SEE

Everybody sees the blind man
    walking down the street,
    tapping his cane,
    stopping at the corner
    wondering about the light.

Everybody sees the man at the office
    intoxicated by his title,
    or liquor,
    or the new secretary.

Everybody sees when a politician
    is feeding us baloney,
    or sees the weird way
    cops give tickets,
    or the injustice of promotions.

Nobody seems to see themselves,
    the way they hurt others,
    or insult others,
    or what's worse
    to completely ignore
    the possibility
    that this other person
    might have something to offer.

Nobody seems to see that there are people out there,
    fathers behind papers,
    wives in the kitchen,
    young men under car hoods,
    people in nursing homes,
    kids watching TV,
    priests after sermons,
    who have been waiting for years
    for us to notice that they exist.

Lord, that I might see.

FRIENDSHIP

Everyone needs the presence
    of a friend,
    for the trip,
    for the journey,
    for the turns along the way.

The wisdom teachers of every generation
    tell us this,
    even though we might run into
    a Judas or a Brutus now and then.

The little kids know it
    as they start out,
    reaching out for friends
    in the playground
    or at school.

The adolescent girls cry,
    as they sit there for hours
    listening to their stereos,
    listening to the latest songs
    about friendship.

The teen-age boys won't use the word
        like the girls do,
        but they too travel in packs,
        and split when it's time
        to have a girl friend.

The married, they say, are lucky
        if the one they marry,
        turns out to be a friend.

Then somehow, somewhere, sometime
        in our thirties,
        we begin to hear
        some inner wisdom
        coming up from the pains of life,
        that friendship is the giving
        and not the getting,
        that friendship is the living
        and even the dying for the other,
        and we wonder why it takes so long
        for all of us to discover this,
        to see for ourselves
        what's on all the cards
        in the card shops,
        to hear from ourselves
        what all the religions
        are trying to teach.

Well, maybe, that's what friends are for.

SHEEP OR GOATS?

Everyone of us knows
        that if the Son of Man,
        the Son of Woman,
        summoned us
        with the sound of the trumpet,
        or the roll of the drums,
        we'd have to be ready
        to give a report
        on how we responded to his call.

Everyone of us knows down deep
        that at the end of our lives
        all of us are going to be called
        before the throne
        to give an account of our stewardship,
        on how we used the gift of life,
        on how we used the gifts of the earth.

Everyone of us knows down deeper
that the Son of Man,
the Son of Women,
comes not with the trumpet,
nor with the roll of the drums,
but that he comes as
The Stranger,
The Hungry,
The Thirsty,
The Naked,
The Sick,
The Prisoner.

And yet, we the children of Man,
the children of Woman,
sit there in our easy chairs,
enjoying our TV,
saying we have no wine,
we have no bread,
we have no room,
we have no time
to take care of Strangers.

And so the Son of Man,
the Son of Woman,
keeps coming to us
in the face of the Stranger,
silently singing his song of love,
silently warning us
that the Neglected
are the judges
who tell us whether the Kingdom has come
into our lives,
telling us whether we are sheep or goats.

PART TWO
Signals

SOUNDS AND SIGNALS

Are you saying what you're saying
or are you saying something else?

We all use words about the weather,
words about sports, food, clothes,
to say "Hello" to another person,
to test the waters,
to find out how the other person
might be feeling that day,
how they sound.

We all do this.

Instead of saying, "I'll miss you,"
we say, "Drive carefully."

Instead of saying, "I'm mad!"
we say, "Put out the garbage."

Instead of saying, "I'm lonely,"
we say, "I'm going to bed."

It's normal.

But are we aware
that we often miss these signals,
these sounds from each other,
sounds that can help us know
what's really going on
inside the other person?

And are we aware that we often miss
these signals because of all the other
conversations that are usually
sounding inside of us?

Why can't we quiet down?
Why can't we get out of ourselves
and begin to hear the heart
of the other person?

Why can't we stop and say,
"Hold it. It sounds to me
that you're trying to say something else.
Are you saying what you're saying
or are you saying something else?"

Why can't we really say,
"I love you,"

or, "I don't feel your love any more,"

or, "Please stay a little longer."

PLEASE POST

If you won't laugh,
you'll have to leave the playground.

If you won't work,
you can't sit at this table.

If you won't pray,
you'll have to leave the church.

If you won't sing,
you'll have to leave the group.

If you won't dance,
you won't be invited to the wedding.

If you won't listen,
you'll end up with a briefcase of only your ideas.

If you won't talk,
you'll have to leave this house.

If you don't vote,
you'll have to stop all that complaining.

If you only buy vanilla, chocolate and strawberry,
you'll never taste chocolate chip ice cream.

If you don't sacrifice,
you'll never know.

If you don't open doors,
you'll never get out.

If you don't get into the boat,
you'll never taste the open sea.

If you are a poor loser,
you can't play cards around here.

If you don't lower your nets,
you'll never make a catch.

If you won't love,
you'll never find God.

ARTIST

All of us search sketch after sketch,
statue after statue,
poem after poem,
in our drive
to picture God.

Creator of heaven and earth,
Giver of breath,
Walker in the garden in the cool of the evening,
Divider of waters,
Judge,
The Great King,
The Most High,
Father of orphans,
Defender of widows,

Lover,
Rock,
Shield,
Mighty Fortress,
Nursing Mother,
Shelter,
Shooter of arrows,
I Am.

And the word became flesh
and dwelt amongst us.

Way,
Truth,
Life,
Door,
Vine,
Living Water,
Living Bread,
Good Shepherd,
Suffering Servant,
Light of the World,
Son of Man.
Son of God.

Before Abraham came to be,
I Am.

And Jesus the Artist said,
"Philip, he who sees me,
sees the Father."

RESURRECTION AND ASCENSION

Everything like bread
is rising,
climbing,
ascending,
reaching
beyond its roots,
its parents.

Everything dies,
becoming
the ground,
the oil,
the coal,
the energy
of future generations.

The seed must die.

The child must leave
            the womb
            and roam
            the earth
            in search
            of love.

The child reaches out
            for food,
            for attention,
            for meaning,
            and hopefully
            will learn
            that he too
            must die
            for others
            if he wants
            to rise
            beyond
            his roots,
            his parents,
            himself.

Everyone must discover
            the path,
            the hill,
            the top,
            the cross,
            and rise
            and ascend
            to ancestors,
            to our Father.

THE CITY OF HAPPY ENDINGS

Everybody longs for The City of Happy Endings,
    where there are no sad stories,
    no slums, no bowery,
    where it's safe to walk
    wherever you want.

Nobody wants to hear about
    unhappy endings,
    that a friend's marriage broke up,
    that a nun lost her faith,
    that a girl had an abortion.

No, we all dream about
    The City of Happy Endings.

And Jesus entered our cities
            and healed our sick,
            the blind and the lame,
            and changed the water into wine,
            giving sad stories
            happy endings.

And Jesus came within sight
            of the city of Jerusalem
            and Jesus wept,
            seeing its unhappy ending.

And Jesus entered that city
            riding on a donkey,
            entered that city
            where he would die,
            suffering an unhappy ending.

But on the third day Jesus rose again
            from the dead,
            he ascended into heaven
            to prepare a place for us.

Therefore everyone can enter the City of God,
            The City of Happy Endings.

I AM HUMAN

I am human—one of us.

I know when I'm on a bridge
and when I'm crossing a river.

I get nervous when I hear the couple in the next house fight,
especially because they have small children.

I get mad at motorcycles when they
roar up my quiet street at midnight.

Sometimes I like rain and sometimes I don't.

I know when I vote and don't vote.

I know when I'm eating watermellon or fresh bread.

I don't know when I'm eating boiled potatoes,
most soups and toast.

I know when someone I love is in the room.

I know when I'm passing a cemetery.

There is something special about horses, especially
when I see a mare and her colt in a green field.

I know when I have a fever or a blister.

When I see a sailboat or a pregnant woman or a church
something happens to me.

I get nervous when I see a person in a wheelchair
or when I see an ambulance flashing
or when a tractor trailor truck is too close.

I slow down, no matter what, when I see a police car.

A baby's fingers always get to me.

I love the ocean.

I feel lonely when I'm in a car alone and there is a couple
close to each other in the car in front of me.

It makes it even worse when certain songs
come over the car radio.

I like it when someone tells me they missed me.

I feel good when I do the same or when I help someone.

Oh yeah, and sometimes I even pray.

ARMS RACE

Winter
afternoon in January,
after a storm,
moving across the world
through small towns,
I am
a slow bus,
vulnerable
to the young hunters,
these future generals
standing on heaps
of dead snow,
arms ready for me to pass.
Why do small boys
throw snow balls
at buses?

THE ONLY SOUND

All of us
have moments
in the night
when we can't sleep,
or moments
when we're scared to sleep,
moments
when our hearts become so loud
it's the only sound
in the whole world
that we hear.

And we begin to fear
that our heart won't go on.

And the beat
becomes a drum,
beating louder and louder,
perhaps because our head
is lying a certain way,
or because of something we ate,
or something we did,
and we're scared
that our heart might stop beating,
that our pulse might end.

And the possibility
of not waking up
in the morning
dawns on us.

And we lie there
in the night
listening,
hoping for the next beat.

And we lie there thinking
about our life.

And suddenly everything
in it becomes secondary.

And only God and the pulsing remain.   103

WHAT'S IMPORTANT?

The teen-ager couldn't wait for summer,
couldn't wait for all those summer mornings
he and his grandfather
went fishing, went talking.

"Grandpa, what's important?"

(LONG PAUSE)

"Well, you'll have to sit back and listen to people
for the answer to that one.

"Or better, you'll have to watch people.
Watch their hands, their faces,
but especially watch their eyes.
People always tell you
what's important with their eyes.

"Why I once had a man tell me that his wife
was dead 3 years and 44 days
and he was still counting,
and his eyes were still crying.

"Or listen to your grandma next time you take
her shopping. Listen to the things
she brings up—the things she talks about
when she meets her friends.
I know you always find shopping
with her boring, but watch her
as she takes out her pictures of you
and all her other grandchildren
to show them to her friends.

"Watch people watch their watches.
They're telling you an awful lot.
And yawns . . . Notice yawns.
They're always a dead give away.

"Listen to the sounds behind words, behind voices . . .
what people get angry at,
when they get mad.
Then you'll know when someone is stepping
on somebody's values or somebody's nerves.
Then you'll know that someone is going beyond
somebody's 'No tresspassing. Private property' sign.

"And don't worry too much about people's answers.
Listen to their questions.
Questions always tell you a lot more."

(LONG PAUSE)

"By the way, why did you ask that question?"

EASTER IS A BURSTING

Jump out of your coffins
Burst through the earth.
Rise in hope you Children of the Light.

Green the earth.
Music the air.
Dawn the darkness wherever you find it.

Nurses in nursing homes,
dance down the corridors.
Make it more than a job.

Secretaries and teachers,
bring some laughter into
all those frozen faces that you see today.

Hope the hopeless.
Joy the joyless.
Tickle them till they smile.

You optometrists, prescribe
rainbow colored glasses
to all those who see everything as sin.

Rejoice with us.
The Lord is with us.
He is risen as He said.

THE TWO HANDS

I am a fist,
      a sign of fear,
      a sign of anger,
      a sign of greed,
      a sign of tension.

      I can pound a desk,
      I can hoard money,
      I can try to scare you,
      I can punch you
          in the mouth.

      I am a fist.

      What do you think of me?

I am an open hand,
      a sign of calm,
      a sign of ease,
      a sign of peace,
      a sign of relaxation.

      I can dial a phone,
      I can shake a hand,
      I can change the diapers,
      I can play cards,
      I can break the bread,
      I can pass the wine,
      I can heal the hurt,
      I can write the poem.

      I am an open hand.

      What do you think of me?

INSIDE STORY

Does everybody want to know if other people
        feel the same way
        as they do?

Is there anybody out there
        who asks the same questions
        I'm asking?

Does everybody look in the mirror
        when nobody is looking,
        and stare deep
        into their eyes
        and wonder all kinds of things?

Does everybody have at least one thing
        they are scared to tell
        anyone else?

Does everybody have doubts about God
       right in the middle
       of a religious service,
       wondering whether this whole thing
       is real . . . wondering whether
       some other religion might have
       more of the TRUTH?

Does everybody find themselves in
       the middle of a job,
       the middle of a marriage,
       the middle of a party,
       the middle of a conversation,
       asking themselves,
       "What am I doing here?"

Does everybody at times wish they were someone else?

Does everybody at times wonder, "Is there anyone out there
       who would want to be me?"

Does everybody have feelings of frustration, or anger,
       or revenge, wanting to get even
       with someone who hurt them,
       who burnt them?

Does everyone spend time wondering what
       other people wonder about?

PRESENCE

Let's be honest.
We all know about presence,
whether a person wants to be with us
or whether they feel trapped,
like a prisoner in our presence.

The baby knows.
She knows even when she's sleeping
whether her parents want her or not.

The old people know.
They know which of their children
are only a phone call
or a visit away.

The team knows whether the cheer leaders
have to cheer or want to cheer.
They know when the crowd
is with them or not.
They know. They can sense it.

The people in the church know
whether the preacher
wants to be in the pulpit or not.

The wife—the husband—they both know
whether their marriage
has become a trap—people living,
people dying in separate prison cells,
or whether their marriage
is an ever expanding universe,
an ever expanding move towards God.

I am.

God is present and we know it.

Presence:
we know these truths about presence
even when we deny them.

And all is touching.
All the cells of the universe
are touching each other,
present to each other,
cheering each other on.

All is present to all.
All is circular.
Everything is present to everything.
Everyone is present to everyone.
Everyone is present to God.

God is present to everyone and everything.
The universe is a sign
of the ever expanding presence of God,
like the baby to the parents.

My life is touching your life.
Life is touching life.
Life is touching God.

Yet some people feel trapped.
They feel like they are dying,
in a closed prison cell,
unable to open up to the presence of another person,
to the presence of God.

And the truth will set you free.

And all cells will be opened.

REALITY THERAPY

Discovering my job
has become more important
than my family.

Planning the whole day
on the way into work,
lining up every minute of it,
only to see the boss
waiting for me
with a piece of paper in his hand
as I walk in the door.

Seeing my son bored
by something that really interests me.

My brother wants to put mom
in a nursing home,
and my sister doesn't
and I'm caught in the middle,
and I'm the only one who has taken care of mom
for the past four years
since she had her stroke.

Finding out I never really knew
my dad till after he died.

Couldn't wait till the talk was over
to complain about it,
only to hear that everybody liked it.

Going to bed on the night
after a funeral
with one less person in the house.

Trying to make a right turn
out of my driveway,
but nobody will let me out.

Finally somebody slows down
and waves for me to pull out
into traffic in front of him.

Finding myself a few seconds later
speeding up to stop somebody else
who is trying to make a right turn
out of their driveway
just as I was.

Looking in the mirror to see
if the person in the car behind me
just saw what I did.

THE JOURNEY

Time,
crawling,
walking,
running,
playing,
entering classrooms,
laughing,
dying for summer,
adolescent feelings,
college or a job,
change,
death and resurrection,
crowded streets,
stopping to look in store windows,
reflections and possibilities,
buying and selling,
jobs,
coming to corners,
STOP,
WALK,
red to green,
a new street,
meeting,
more feelings,
you,
you,

rejections and being rejected,
mistakes,
finally meeting that one person
who means everything in life,
feeling complete,
illusions,
passing churches till I was 38,
then sitting in the back
of dark churches
for the next few years,
finally joining the congregation,
feeling phony for a while,
then slowly realizing
we're only children putting on a play,
newer temptations,
these more serious,
and deeper inside me,
more and more finding myself looking backwards,
trying to figure out my parents,
slowly,
my children leaving home,
my wife and I alone once again,
death,
more and more sickness,
getting slower,
and slower.
STOP,
WALK,
red to green,
a new street,
wondering what's next.

PERCEPTION

Is what you see
what it is?

If I say she's pretty,
is she pretty?

What about ugliness?

Who decides?

Who decides who can cast the stones?

Who appoints who's to be the judge;
who appoints who's to be the jury?

Who gives the poem depth;
the reader of the writer?

Are there any little people?

What is good music?

In one apartment it's good music
and it's all part of the party,
while in the next apartment
it's noise coming through the walls,
disturbing the peace,
disturbing our sleep.

Sleep.

It's always night somewhere.

Yet the sun is always shining.

The sun is always rising
somewhere around the world.

Awake!

Little people around the world awake!

Rise!

Shine!

Put down your stones.

Stop being judge and jury.

See beyond the walls of your apartment.

See the beauty, the music, the poetry
surrounding you,
always rising,
all around the world.

PLEASE CHECK ONE

I didn't start living:

    ____ till I hit 40.

    ____ till I hit 60.

    ____ till I had a heart attack.

    ____ till I learned to laugh at myself.

    ____ till I quit the rat race.

    ____ till I met my wife.

_____ till I realized I was still
competing against my brother.

_____ till I got over trying to please
my father.

_____ till I became a parent.

_____ till my husband and I realized
we got married for all the wrong reasons,
had a crisis, and at the kitchen table
we had a long late night conversation
and remarried each other.

_____ till I hit bottom.

_____ till I had a long talk with someone
who knew how to listen and helped me see
what I really wanted to do with my life.

_____ till I decided there were things that I
could do, and do well, and that I don't have
to put myself down for not going to college.

_____ till God came into my life.

_____ none of the above.

STUCK

Part of us
      is a garbage can
      taking up space
      somewhere inside us,
      probably in our cellar.

And at times
      we can't wait
      to put our garbage can
      out on the sidewalk.

We can't wait for the garbage man
      to come along and dump the whole mess.

And we can't wait
        to hear the hollow sound
        of the garbage can
        banging its way back to the sidewalk,
        empty.

And then we bring it back to our cellar.

But what bothers us
        is that some of the garbage
        always seems to remain:
        a tea bag,
        some decaying meat,
        clinging to our insides.

Resentments,
        unforgiven remarks,
        memories of sins,
        the stink of our life,
        stuck inside us,
        keeping us humble,
        knowing that we too
        have made mistakes,
        forgotten others,
        said the wrong words,
        failed,
        and the Lord loves us just the same
        in spite of our garbage,
        in spite of our stink.

PRAYER

Prayer is a hungering,
    a thirsting,
    the hunt,
    the journey.

Prayer is not noise,
    nor silence,
    the slot machine,
    the twisting of God's arm.

Prayer is not numbers,
    nor mere words,
    the self-satisfiers,
    or the God avoiders.

Prayer is moments on knees,
    moments of "time out",
    the wrestling,
    then the burst of joy.

HANDICAP

What's the worst handicap?

Is it blindness, deafness,
    or being paralyzed?

Is it self-pity—giving up even in oneself?

Is it losing part of oneself,
    for example, a leg, a friend
    or a wife?

Is it being paralyzed by a sin
        like jealousy, or anger,
        or the inability to forgive,
        freezing us for a week,
        or even for the whole winter?

Is it the inability to see our brother
        at our door, needing our help,
        needing food, needing our care?

Is it alcoholism or drug addiction?

Or is it being caught up in the rapids
        of lust or money or fame?

Is it the inability of seeing other people
        as different—being wrapped too tightly
        in oneself?

Or is it the inability to believe in God,
        in life,
        in the Kingdom,
        both here and hereafter?

Or is it the disability of pride,
        not knowing we have handicaps
        but knowing that others do?

What is the worst handicap?

FATHER'S DAY

Father,
the word
we use to describe
not only our dad,
but also our God.

Father,
the one
who got up every morning
for all those years
to work hard
to give us
our daily bread.

Father,
the one
who waited
with hidden feelings,
because men weren't supposed
to show their emotions,
for our first step,
for our first word,
for our first report card,
our first date,
our first job,
our first child.

Father,
the one
who like God
taught us
strength,
forgiveness,
quiet,
respect,
and a hundred other virtues
we never knew he had.

Father,
the one
who secretly
waited   .
for Father's Day.

35TH BIRTHDAY

By the time you hit your 35th birthday
you'd better know:

1) Why some people enjoy fishing
and why some enjoy knitting.

2) The importance of keeping one's word.

3) How to listen and how to smile.

4) What people in their 60's go through.

5) The step in life that comes after idealism.

6) What money can and can't buy.

7) Whether you learn more from pleasure or from pain.

8) That everyone makes mistakes and has skeletons in their closet.

9) Why we need vacations, holidays, special days, Saturdays and Sundays.

10) The importance of clapping when a kid writes his name for the first time and to keep on asking him to write it till his legs stop clapping too.

11) The beginning of adult religion in my life.

12) The importance of sorting out just who my parents were and what made them tick and how I fit into the family along with any brothers and sisters.

13) That there are people in the world suffering from hunger, sin and all kinds of injustice.

14) That it's the person behind the person who counts.

15) Death is a possibility.

LITANY FOR PENTECOST

Our homes,
our schools,
our churches are all dead.

Come Holy Spirit.

The bulb is out.
The thermostat won't work.
The fireplace is cold.

Come Holy Spirit.

We're ships
that are standing still
with sails that have given up hope.

Come Holy Spirit.

We're windmills
that have forgotten
how to turn.

Come Holy Spirit.

Be a wind;
roar across the waters
and fill our sails.

Come Holy Spirit.

Be a fire
that will melt all the ice
and snow that is clinging to us.

Come Holy Spirit.

Be the bird that brings
the olive branch back to the ark
when we're saying, "There is no hope."

Come Holy Spirit.

FAITH, HOPE AND CHARITY

Faith is a letting go,
        a surrender,
        to mystery,
        to sickness,
        to death,
        to resurrection,
        to God.

        It means
        becoming a chalice
        when God is pouring,
        leaving home
        when God is calling,
        letting go
        when God is pulling.

Hope is a knowing,
        a trusting
        in the not yet,
        to what's around the corner,
        to the night,
        to the next day.

        It means
        opening the present
        before receiving it,
        hearing God
        without hearing him,
        setting sail
        with another's map.

Love is a reaching out,
        a noticing,
        a serving,
        a dying,
        a rising,
        to another,
        to the needy,
        to the pain,
        to the lonely,
        to the loved one.

        It means
        setting no limits,
        accepting inconvenience
        to help the inconvenient,
        knowing that one's life
        is meant for more.

RETREAT

Feeling tired,

Feeling older,

Feeling that you're losing your touch,

Realizing that the fat is winning,

Getting anxious,

Trouble sleeping,

Noise starting to get to you,

Can't keep up with the others,

Seems like the world is passing you by,

Neglecting the people you are living with,

Feeling guilty,

Don't know what's next,

Retreat,

Escape,

To the desert,

To the mountains,

To the water,

Find a quiet place,

Sit by the river,

Reflect,

Start to pray,

Root yourself in the Soil of God,

Return home

With perspective,

Refreshed,

Jesus did.

THE LATEST FASHION

What this world needs
        is a change of heart
        and not of garments.

Yet pick up any newspaper
        and you'll see
        story after story
        of selfishness
        and corruption,
        followed by
        page after page
        of the latest fashions.

It must be basic human nature then
        to clean the outside of the cup
        instead of the inside,
        to want to have new clothes
        instead of a new heart.

We don't need fashion plates.

We need people who will start worrying
        about all the rest of the people
        on the island,
        who will stop all their grumbling,
        stop exploiting the poor,
        stop polluting the air and the water,
        taking, taking, taking,
        wasting, wasting, wasting.

We need people who will start with themselves,
        parents who will be parents,
        mothers who will learn to let go,
        so their kids can become adults.

We need people who will communicate with love,
        instead of using guilt and fear
        to motivate people.

In other words, as Jesus said,
        "Stop picking up the newspaper
        or watching television in order
        to complain about the world.
        Complain about yourself to yourself.
        Change your heart and stop worrying
        about your garments."

THE CHRISTMAS WAITING

The leaves have long gone,
      leaving behind empty branches,
      dark and barren
      against December skies,
      trees standing there,
      arms outstretched,
      waiting,
      waiting. . . .

The shoppers stand there,
      arms full of presents,
      hoping that these clothes,
      these toys, these gifts,
      will bring joy to the world
      of their loved ones,
      who are waiting,
      waiting. . . .

The kids' imaginations are expanding,
      picturing bigger and better dolls,
      stranger and stranger creatures
      from outer space,
      with rocket powered fists,
      and battery powered eyes,
      as they sit there in classrooms
      planning the 12 days of Christmas,
      waiting,
      waiting. . . .

The Salvation Army with red ribbons and bright smiles
     stand there in the cold
     with jingle bells,
     waiting,
     waiting. . . .

Stores with extra help and extra merchandise
     stand there
     waiting,
     waiting. . . .

Choirs practice extra sessions,
     extra evenings,
     waiting,
     waiting. . . .

Wait a minute!

Maybe this year I'll make room in my inn;
     maybe this year
     I'll open my door
     and let Christ in,
     who for all these years
     has been standing there
     outside my life,
     arms full of gifts,
     waiting,
     waiting. . . .

A NEW YEAR

Happy New Year!

Maybe this year I'll be happy.
Maybe this year things will be better.

Starting again . . .
Isn't that the feeling that hugs everyone
as the old year fades,
as the new year invades us?

It's almost midnight . . .
5 . . . 4 . . . 3 . . . 2 . . . 1 . . .
Happy New Year!

A new year . . . a new me!

Resolutions:
This year I resolve
to lose 15 pounds.
This year I resolve
to spend more time with the kids.
This year I resolve
to spend more time with God,
to start praying again.

But then I sober up.
By January 4th I'll probably
be back to my old tricks.
I'll be like a stale jelly donut.
On January 1st I'm fresh, brand new,
just in from the bakery,
but four days later . . .
the same old me . . .
a stale jelly donut.

Jesus, why does this happen every year?
Why do I make all these fresh resolutions
at the start of every year,
and then four days later
it's the same old me?

Is it because I'm trying to pour
new wine into old wine skins,
new jelly into stale jelly donuts,
making big promises with my mouth,
without any real change of heart?

Is it because I try to keep
all these promises on my own,
forgetting you are with me
all days, that is, if I want to have a
Happy New Year?

MARRIAGE: HOPES AND PROMISES

Today you are going to be married.

Today you are going to make deep promises to each other.

Hopes and promises.

High hopes for both of you—
        rather,
        deep hopes.

Deep hopes because each person
        is like a mine
        with untapped treasures
        deep below the surface,
        deep below the skin.

Hopes that you'll never give up on each other,
        that you'll keep on working,
        keep on mining,
        that you'll always be faithful
        to your promise to try to bring out
        the unique treasures
        that God has placed within each person
        for the wealth of the world.

Perhaps it will be a precious sense of humor,
        or the strength of iron,
        or the softness of gold,
        or the imagination of aluminum,
        metals you'll discover
        in your mines,
        metals we hope will endure
        on through your silver
        and golden anniversaries.

Hopes that you know that marriage
        is hard work, like
        running a mine.
        You'll have to build foundations,
        structures and supports for each other.
        You'll have to take risks, cross fingers,
        but especially pray for each other
        as you go deeper and deeper
        into the inner caves of each other.

Hopes that you realize that running a mine
        is a marriage of hopes and experience,
        taking chances but learning from experience.

Hopes that you're aware that some mines go on strike
        and some mines fail.

Will yours?

We're all here today to say and to pray, "We hope not."

THE KINGDOM OF STUFF

Most of us are citizens
   of the Kingdom of Stuff.

We're overloaded:
   our wires,
   our cars,
   our closets,
   our stomachs,
   our lives.

There are so many plugs,
   so many wires in our electrical outlets
   that we always pull out the wrong one
   when we want to bring the portable TV
   into the kitchen for supper.

We don't want to miss anything.

We want to have everything.

Our suitcases won't close,
   so we go out and buy bigger ones,
   and then we build bigger airplanes.

We dash around in the Kingdom of Stuff,
   driving full speed ahead,
   wasting time,
   wasting fuel,
   wasting our lives,
   looking for the latest gadgets,
   the latest stuff.

We don't know how to cut,
   to reduce the budget,
   to trim the fat out of our lives.

No wonder we can't get through
   the eye of the needle.
   No wonder we don't know anything
   about the Kingdom of God,
   about prayer and service.
   No wonder we don't believe
   that there is a vast sky of possibilities
   on the other side of the needle.

We can't fit.

We refuse to sell what we have and give it to the poor.
   No, we keep speeding down our eight lane highway
   playing our stereos, playing our song,
   "Happy are the rich, the Kingdom of Stuff is theirs."

We speed by Jesus coming up the narrow road,
   riding on a donkey, singing,
   "Happy are the poor in spirit,
   the Kingdom of God is theirs."

God emptied himself. He gave up everything
   to come through the eye of the needle,
   to come into the Kingdom of Stuff.

He walked around telling people to empty their lives,
   empty their suitcases,
   in fact to get rid of them
   "no traveling bags",
   and begin walking the narrow road
   through the eye of the needle
   into the Kingdom of God.

GREEN IVY

Everybody stops—
    to watch
    the parade,
    the reds,
    the whites,
    the blues,

    the bands,
    the floats,
    the aluminum-foilded youth
    marching by . . .

    the
      fading
        from
          the
            picture. . . .

But nobody stops—
    to notice
    the creeping,
    the green,
    the old ivy,
    the clinging,
    the gradual
    destruction
    of the building
    on the street
    the youth marched down. . . .